Powerful Praise Worthy Worship

Shiela Y. Harris

Roosevelt T. Harris
(Deceased)

Copyright © 2013 Shiela Y. Harris
All rights reserved.
ISBN-978-09679312-6-5

Unless otherwise indicated all scripture notations are taken from the Holy Bible, New International Version ® Copyright © 1973, 1978, 1984 by International Bible Society. Used by permission of Zondervan Publishing House, All rights reserved.

The "NIV" and "New International Version" trademarks are registered in the United States Patent and Trademark Office by the International Bible Society. Use of either trademark requires permission of International Bible Society.

Scripture quotations marked KJV are taken from the King James Version of the Bible.

All rights reserved. No part of this publication may be reproduced, stored in a retrieval system or transmitted in any form or by any means, electronic, mechanical, photocopying, recording or otherwise, without written consent from the author or publisher.

DEDICATION

To my wonderful mentors Pastors, Melvin and April Jackson for introducing us to and teaching us the art and ministry of praise and worship…"Morning Glory," and to
Bishop Sheridan and First Lady LarLeslie McDaniel for their legacy of presenting worship to produce worshippers.

CONTENTS

Chapter		Page No.
	Acknowledgments	7
	Introduction	9
	Forward	11
1	The Difference Between Praise and Worship	13
2	Praise	17
3	The Seven Levels of Praise	19
4	Worship is a Lifestyle	23
5	Minister or Director of Music	29
6	Worship Leader	33
7	Worship Team	37
8	Musicians	41
9	Praise and Worship Service	43
10	Praise and Worship Enhancements	47
	Synopsis	51
	About the Author	
	Other Teaching Topics	

ACKNOWLEDGMENTS

This book is the project of the late
Pastor Roosevelt "Ted" Harris III but God called him home before
he could complete it. I made a vow to complete the work and the
promise has been kept.

1957 - 2007

Introduction

As I edited and completed this book I wept tears of joy. For many years the late Pastor Ted and I taught, lived, and breathed praise and worship and church administration. As a team, we opened many services with praise and worship and taught seminars in numerous venues.

In 2003, Pastor Ted began writing a book on the art and ministry of praise and worship but he made his heavenly transition before it could be completed. This work is a compilation of the work he started and all the information we gathered over years of study and teaching. My God, what a journey!

It is with great excitement but more importantly I am eternally grateful for our spiritual covering at that time, under Grace Unlimited Ministries (formally known as Believers' Christian Fellowship) with Pastors Melvin and April Jackson. Their phenomenal teachings and lifestyle introduced us to Praise and Worship, tithes and offering and the ministry of the Holy Spirit, all which incredibly CHANGED OUR LIVES.

Prior to our uniting with the Jackson's, the music experience was choir selections, congregational and devotional singing all which gave us foundation. I am honored and elated that Pastor Jackson wrote the forward for this work, giving me pointers and for his overall collaboration with me on this project. Years of research and scripted materials we've used for teaching praise and worship are included in this work. May this book inform, enhance, encourage and empower your praise and worship experience.

Forward

Ted and Shiela Harris (former choir directors and executive pastors) are two people I am very fond of and grateful for their works and service in our ministry. I first met them both working diligently in their separate choir workshops. His was G.M.I.W. (Gospel Music and Instructional Workshop) and hers was Y.P.M.I.W. (Young People's Music and Instructional Workshop). It was in these workshops that I even got the chance to introduce my original songs I had written over the years.

But as I remember, I also had the opportunity to see them transition from choir conductors into "worshipers". Now to some, this may not present a difference. For, in my mind, anyone can sing a song well. Choir décor is considerably important, but "worship" holds greater, because it "costs you something". David would *not even* accept a parcel of land freely offered to him, simply because in his refusal he said, "I *must* pay (give, offer) something to worship." This is why after having read its contents; this book has won a special place in my heart.

I believe it purposes to serve as a brief guide in helping Pastors who are trying to develop and build a Praise and Worship ministry. It is also a great resource for those aspiring to become Praise and Worship leaders.

Let's remember, talent alone is not enough. .."They that worship Him *must* worship Him in spirit and truth." (John 4:24)

Pastor Melvin O. Jackson
Grace Unlimited Ministries, Los Angeles CA

Chapter One

THE DIFFERENCE BETWEEN PRAISE AND WORSHIP

Praise and worship are not simply a song service or a period to express spiritual emotions, but is a distinct art and lifestyle. It is an intimacy one achieves only through being in right standing with God and knowing what God's desire is for His people through the art of praise and worship. Knowing the purpose for praise and worship catapults and perpetuates healing and deliverance while taking us right into the throne room of God. Selah (Think about it).

Praise is defined in the English language, to express a favorable Judgment of: to glorify (a god or a saint) an expression of approval.

Praise defined in Greek, the predominant language of the New Testament is *Epainos* meaning praise or to bestow commendation, it is used on account of, and by reason of God's heritage. This kind of "praise" is to be ascribed only to God, in respect to His character and operations. If He never does anything else He's still worthy to be praised!

As with anything there are some discrepancies regarding how we should praise. Some confuse it or even mix it with devotion. In a devotional service the songs are styled more for congregational singing often sung using a hymnal. Its purpose is not necessarily to get to the throne room of God or to make any distinction between praise and worship but moreover to sing hymns with several verses and a chorus usually without a team or leader. Instrumentation used in earlier times posed another problem. Some traditional services preferred the use of a piano and organ only.

Psalm 150 reads:

Praise ye the LORD. Praise God in his sanctuary: praise him in the firmament of his power. Praise him for his mighty acts: praise him according to his excellent greatness. Praise him with the sound of the trumpet: praise him with the psaltery and harp. Praise him with the timbrel and dance: praise him with stringed instruments and organs. Praise him upon the loud cymbals: praise him upon the high sounding cymbals. Let everything that hath breath praise the LORD. Praise ye the LORD.

This psalm was primarily intended for the Levites, to stir them up to walk in their office in the house of the Lord, as singers and players on instruments. Yet, we must take it as speaking to us, who are reaching out to our God as spiritual priests today. This entire Psalm is an exhortation to praise the Lord! Once we leave the realm of praise and enter into worship we should also be careful not to intertwine the two or return to praise.

Worship defined in English is to ascribe, to attribute, assign, or give credit, worth or value, or to count worthy. When we worship God, we acknowledge that He is. We acknowledge 'WHO" He is and "WHAT" He is. Worship = Worth-ship.

Our worship does not make Him worthy – We worship Him because He already is worthy! *"Worship"* defined in the Greek is *"proskuneo."* It means to reverence or to kiss so worship involves intimacy. This is one of the reasons we do not clap during the worship period of our "praise and worship" service.

Some years ago, my late husband and I were challenged in a meeting as to whether there was any definitive scripture for clapping being inappropriate during worship. In examining specific acts of worship in the Scriptures, we see there are a variety of expressions and postures. What we did not do in that meeting, will not be done in this book. It is not written to conjure arguments or incite debates but moreover to help the readers have the best worship experience possible.

We can all agree on scripture commanding that we worship God and that we exalt His name and offer Him our sacrifice of praise. There is biblical proof for both the lifting of hands as an act of worship and the clapping of hands as an act of praise.

<u>Psalms 47:1</u> *says, "Clap your hands, all you nations; shout to God with cries of joy."* In this instance, it's praise because it is shouts of joy. Both clapping and shouting out joyful worship to God are urged.

In <u>1Timothy 2:8</u> we read "I want men everywhere to lift up holy hands in prayer, without anger or disputing."

The attitude of the heart is emphasized in this verse. But also seen is that lifting hands is an appropriate posture.

Making the posture distinction between the two and because the Greek word for Worship is "Prokuneo" meaning to kiss, this encompasses intimacy and therefore not clapping certainly changes and sets the atmosphere for getting into the presence of God. Having experienced the gesture of worship with and without clapping; the lifting of hands has always set a "with one accord" atmosphere.

We must have a true relationship with God if we expect to have any chance at worshipping Him. We cannot fool God with false intimacy. If we are not in right standing with God, He absolutely will know it. You can sing twenty songs, say "come on worshippers" thirty times and do forty note runs, but if there is no intimacy in our personal time and lifestyle – baby, it ain't happenin'.

God wants to be intimate with us and some of us are still trying to figure out His phone number. God wants to be intimate with us and some of us are still trying to figure out how to take Him out to dinner. God wants our whole body, soul (mind intellect and emotions), and spirit, it all belongs to Him anyway.

Praise is always <u>exclamatory</u> and worship is always <u>reverent</u>. In praise, we are always talking <u>about</u> God and in worship; we are always talking <u>to</u> God. In praise, we are <u>boasting</u> about God and in worship, we are being <u>intimate</u> with God. In praise, we use our hands to clap. In Worship, we lift our hands because of the intimacy and expressed reverence.

<u>*John 4:23-24*</u>

But the hour cometh, and now is, when the true worshippers shall worship the Father in spirit and in truth: for the Father seeketh such to worship him. God is a Spirit: and they that worship him must worship him in spirit and in truth.

To worship in spirit means to be concerned with and knowledgeable of spiritual realities, not in outward sacrifices, cleansings and trappings. To worship in truth means we worship according to the wholeness of God's Word, especially in light of the New Testament revelation. It's not in our dress or pious mannerisms but distinctive by our pureness of heart.

Worship sometimes seems more like a segment of entertainment. But there has been, and will be a remnant of worshippers that worship Him in spirit and in truth. God's Word implies He is seeking such worshippers. No matter how some may try to glamorize worship, God is in all ages gathering into Himself a generation of true, spiritual worshippers.

A serious problem in our twenty-first century church is we incorporated praise and worship into our service as though it were a new trend. Some have transitioned from devotion and congregational singing to praise and worship (which is often intertwined) without drawing a distinction between the two or grasping a true understanding of its purpose.

Praise and Worship is not just an expression or emotion. Choosing to praise and worship God with our whole heart – is to draw nearer or closer to Him. The whole of man is involved in true and pure praise and worship. Praise and Worship is not something we do as a hobby – IT IS A LIFESTYLE!

Chapter Two

PRAISE

We praise Him because of his wondrous works. We praise Him because of His grace and mercy towards us and we praise God to get results. With our praise, obedience to God, and our pleasing life style, when we praise God we can expect to get results!

Pure praise is the direct phone call that gets God immediately involved in our dilemmas and our situations. The Bible says in Psalm 22:3 the Lord inhabits (or enthrones) the praises of His people. When we praise Him, we can expect to find Him giving us – RESULTS!

We praise God for the victory *(2 Corinthians 2:14):*

Now thanks be unto God, which always causeth us to triumph in Christ, and maketh manifest the savour of his knowledge by us in every place

We may not see the manifestation but God has already caused us to triumph, so we praise Him for it - Now!

Hebrew 13:15-16

Therefore by Him let us continually offer the sacrifice of praise to God, that is, the fruit of our lips, giving thanks to His name. But do not forget to do good and to share, for with such sacrifices God is well pleased.

We do not have altars as in the Old Testament but we have the cross and our High Priest is Jesus Christ. Our sacrifice is not the death of an animal as with the old covenant but the sacrifice of praise from the fruit of our lips.

Praise that truly pleases God is offered continually to Him. Praise that pleases God is a sacrifice in that it may be costly or inconvenient. Praise that pleases God is the fruit of our lips; it is spoken out unto the Lord, either in prose or in song. What proceeds from the lips is regarded as fruit, and fruit reveals the character of its source, as the fruit of a tree reveals the nature of the tree.

Praise is not the only sacrifice that pleases God. When we do good and share that is a sacrifice that pleases God. Praise and worship are important, but our obligations as Christians do not end there.

The reason we worship God is because of WHO He is! Not because we want something, but because of WHO He is! We worship Him for who He is and for his attributes. Without Him we have nothing, will be nothing and simply – are nothing. That is why we worship Him.

Praise says we recognize who God is, but worship says we love that which we recognize. Worship is the vehicle that gets us into the throne room of God. That is the ultimate goal of any praise and worship service, to get to where God is so we can kiss his face.

High praise is an ostentatious celebration with the people and musicians. We can find ourselves clapping, dancing, waving, jumping, running and shouting with great excitement.

We should never have to be prompt, primed or feel as though we are doing God a favor. We should never allow anyone or any situation (including ourselves) to keep us from praising God. In everything, give God thanks, not because of everything, but in everything. DO NOT UNDERESTIMATE PRAISE! IT – IS – POWERFUL!

> I will praise thee, O LORD, with my whole heart; I will show forth all thy marvelous works. I will be glad and rejoice in thee; I will sing praise to thy name, O thou most High. Psalm 9:1

Chapter Three

THE SEVEN LEVELS OF PRAISE

The bible has seven Hebrew words that mean praise and is referred to as the seven levels of praise. Though each is distinctive they also parallel the other and are often combined.

Towdah: Means to "extend the hands" (with the palms up) in a sacrifice of praise, thanksgiving, or thank offering. By raising our hands it as if we are in a court of law and we are speaking truth, and speaking the same thing. Jesus is the sacrifice that we confess with. We are thanking God for what we have on hand and for what we are about to receive. Reference Psalm 50:23:

"Whoso offereth praise glorifieth me: and to him that ordereth his conversation aright will I shew the salvation of God.

Psalm 50:14
Offer unto God praise (Towdah) and pay the vows unto the most High.

Yadah: Means to praise with extended hands, to throw or thrust out the hands to give thanks to God. In Yadah we have the extending of our hands that most of us are familiar with. When we can go beyond ourselves and our circumstances, reaching towards God we give Yadah to God. Reference Psalm 22:22; Psalm 63:5

2 Chronicles 20:21

Give thanks (yadah) to the Lord, for His loving kindness is everlasting.

Halah: Derived from the word Hallelujah. Halah means to laud, to boast, to celebrate, to appear ravenously or clamorously foolish. The celebration would be the same as you were enthusiastically cheering on your favorite sports team when they are winning. Additional scripture references are: Psalm 104-106; 2 Chronicles 20:19-21; Psalm 22:22-26 and Psalm 111:1-3.

Psalm 149:3

Let them praise his name in the dance: let them sing praises unto him with the timbrel and harp.

Shabach: To address in a loud tone, it is the exclamatory form of praise. When you Shabach the Lord, there is a loud testimonial shout to what God has done. We find this illustrated in:

Psalm 47:1 117:1:

O clap your hands, all peoples; shout (shabach) unto God with a voice of triumph.

Zamar: It means to pluck the strings of an instrument, to sing, to praise. It is a musical word and is largely involved with joyful expressions of music, accompanied by the voice singing praise to the accompaniment of musical instruments.

Zamar is the most dominate musical verb In the Hebrew language throughout the Psalms. It was an expression of praise and worship music used in the Old Testament. A popular Psalm that was set to music is Psalm 150.

Psalm 57:8-9

Awake up, my glory; awake, psaltery and harp: I [myself] will awake early. I will praise thee, O Lord, among the people: I will sing unto thee among the nations.

Barak: To express the attitude of love through kneeling, to bless. It's to salute or to kneel in adoration, to declare God the origin of power for success and prosperity. To acknowledge that God is who He is – God! This is used throughout the Old Testament. David shows us how to bless God in Psalm 95:6:

Oh come let us worship and bow down let us kneel (Barak) before the Lord our maker.

Other scripture to reference are: Judges 5:2; Psalm 16:7; Psalm 34:1; Psalm 66:8; Psalm 100:4; Psalm 103; Psalm 113: and Psalm 96:2.

Tehillah: A derivative of the Hebrew word Halal. It is generally accepted to mean the singing of Halal's. To boast about Him in words and music.

Psalm 22:3 is a good example.

But thou art holy, O thou that inhabitest the praises of Israel.

This is an unrehearsed unprepared singing better known as "singing in the spirit." A clearer definition of the word is simply **to sing until we get drunk in the spirit.**

"It is our mandate

To

Present Worship

And Produce Worshipers.

We believe that the

Position of Worship

Is our Position to Receive."

So…we stay in position,

With hands and lives uplifted.

Bishop Sheridan E. McDaniel
Former pastor of
Worship Center Community Church
Long Beach, California

Chapter Four

WORSHIP IS A LIFESTYLE

Worship is an act of obedience to God. God responds with His presence when we open up to Him with all our heart, soul and mind. We should not just strive to be in God's presence corporately on Sunday but in our secret places daily that are only known to you and Him.

From my very first introduction to cooperate praise and worship I've had an unquenchable desire to be in God's presence. It is incredible to dwell in His presence and be lost in time and space; to be saturated by His power and love is almost uncontainable and inexpressible.

Worship is so much more than songs, runs and riffs. If we do not worship God, who is *a spirit, in the spirit,* we cannot *give him the glory due to his name,* and cannot expect to obtain His favor and unfortunately what we are calling worship is for naught.

Late one evening, while flipping through channels on the television I came across a Chinese service. The worship team was singing a song with and the lyrics were…"I will choose Christ, I will choose love, You are my source, You are my Healer, awesome God you are…" English and Chinese subtitles were on the screen and so I paused. Neither voices nor harmony were the greatest but the message and spirit of worship was clear. The accompaniment was complimentary, and audience was receptive with hands lifted. In my amazement the entire worship ministered to me in both languages. I found myself sitting in front of the television, hands lifted and tears streaming. Awesome God!

Though many a corrupt life has perverted the act of worship, we cannot continually live unholy lives, while participating in immoral activities and frequenting unholy places only to show up for Sunday service declaring to be a worshipper. This is unacceptable.

In Isaiah 58 we find God exposes the shallow worship if His people.

Isaiah 58:13-14 (NIV)

"Keep the Sabbath day holy. Don't pursue your own interests on that day, but enjoy the Sabbath and speak of it with delight as the LORD's holy day. Honor the Sabbath in everything you do on that day, and don't follow your own desires or talk idly. Then you shall delight yourself in the LORD; And I will cause you to ride on the high hills of the earth, And feed you with the heritage of Jacob your father. The mouth of the LORD has spoken."

Am I saying Christians are required to keep the Sabbath today? No. The New Testament makes it clear that Christians are not under obligation to observe a Sabbath day, this has been fulfilled by Jesus. Galatians 4:10 tells us that Christians are not bound to observe *days and months and seasons and years.* The rest we experience and enter into as Christians is something to experience every day, not just one day a week - the rest of knowing we don't have to work to save ourselves, but that our salvation was accomplished in Jesus death and resurrection.

The meaning of the Sabbath should not be kept merely as an empty religious ritual, but it and all days should be used to delight ourselves in the LORD. Here God exposed the emptiness of two religious rituals as practiced in Isaiah's day: fasting and Sabbath keeping. Both of these are expressions of not doing things. In fasting, you don't eat. In Sabbath keeping, you don't work. An important aspect to this chapter is showing us that what we don't do isn't enough to make us right before God. Our worship and walk with God shouldn't only be defined by what we don't do but in what we do for the Lord being manifested in our lives before Him daily.

The reason we worship God is because of WHO He is! Not because we want something, but because of WHO He is! We worship Him for who He is and his according to His many attributes. Without Him we have nothing, will be nothing and simply – are nothing. That is why we worship Him.

Praise says we recognize who God is, but worship says we love that which we recognize. Worship is the vehicle that gets us into the throne room of God. That is the ultimate goal of any praise and worship service, to get into the presence of God so we can kiss his face.

It is not a time for testimonies (from the leader or the congregation). It is not a time for us to ask God for anything. (Remember: everything at this time is about God, not about us). It is not a time for a lot of talking and introduction. Worship will cost you something. Our worship is not something we can pull on and take off like a dusty old sweater. Our worship will cost us time in prayer, time in consecration, time in fasting and time in reading the Word. Our Worship is worth something, it is valuable.

<u>1 Chronicles 21:18-24</u>

Then the angel of the LORD *commanded Gad to say to David, that David should go up, and set up an altar unto the* LORD *in the threshing floor of Ornan the Jebusite. And David went up at the saying of Gad, which he spake in the name of the* LORD. *And Ornan turned back, and saw the angel; and his four sons with him hid themselves. Now Ornan was threshing wheat. And as David came to Ornan, Ornan looked and saw David, and went out of the threshing floor, and bowed himself to David with [his] face to the ground. Then David said to Ornan, Grant me the place of this threshing floor, that I may build an altar therein unto the* LORD: *thou shalt grant it me for the full price: that the plague may be stayed from the people. And Ornan said unto David, Take [it] to thee, and let my lord the king do [that which is] good in his eyes: lo, I give [thee] the oxen [also] for burnt offerings, and the threshing instruments for wood, and the wheat for the meat offering; I give it all. And King David said to Ornan, Nay; but I will verily buy it for the full price: for I will not take [that] which [is] thine for the* LORD, *nor offer burnt offerings without cost.*

This is very significant to the cost of worship. Here David meets the Angel of the LORD, and God changed His mind about the plague before it came upon Jerusalem. Now God wanted David to meet Him there in worship. Ornan's threshing floor had a rich history and future. It was on the same hill Abraham was to sacrifice Isaac and the same hill Jesus dies on the cross. Ornan was a generous good hearted man and wanted to give the property to David. But David knew that it would not be a true sacrifice unto God if it did not cost him something. He didn't look for an economic way to please God and it should be the same for us. Our worship should cost us something.

Our pure worship (worship with a true heart and spirit) will usher in the presence of God. Our God will not abide in a house of sin just as most would not want to live in a dusty, dirty, smelly old house. Our cost may be giving up acquaintances, but this will become very easy when we realize the value of our worship. We may have to go through trials from time to time, but this too will become so much easier when we realize that these trials only intensify our praise "and" our worship.

Worship is not a time to call people to the altar for prayer or a time to preach. It is not a time to give harmonic parts or present a concert. No matter what we have written down to sing, the purpose of this time is to usher in the presence of God. Once He honors us with His presence it is not necessary to transition to another song nor is there a need to continue singing everything we have prepared to sing. When we are expecting a guest in our home, once they arrive we don't need to keep calling their cell phone asking them to hurry up and get here. So it is with God, when He arrives bask in His glory.

We have inalienable rights as Worshippers. They include the right to worship God without someone walking over, reaching over or talking over us during the worship period, because this is the most intimate time of the service. We have the right to receive the best from our Praise and Worship leaders and teams, believing their lifestyles are pleasing to God, and they have spent time in prayer and rehearsals to be the best that they can be, even before they ever sing a note before us.

We have the right to not have the praise and worship leader or team "experiment" or practice on us by trying out songs they really have not learned well in their rehearsal. We have the right to not be preached to, because we realize that this time is strictly being observed to give God our deepest and most sincere adulation, reverence, and love - our worship.

We have the right to not be confused by someone telling us to "praise Him" while we are in the middle of "worship", or someone telling us to "worship Him" while we are in the middle of "praise."
We have the right not to have to sing songs that are neither, "praise nor worship," songs that are actually testimonial, congregational, spirituals, or inspirational songs.

True praise and worship begins in the spirit of man and is governed by the will of man. This means one may decide, whether or not to praise or worship God. This is another reason we have so many spectators during the worship time because the choice is ours to make.

Let's not make the error of becoming so modern in the twenty-first century that we forget the importance of reverencing God. It is a wonderful and spiritually exhilarating experience when the ultimate expectation of worshippers is to get to the throne room of God.

Chapter Five

MINISTER OR DIRECTOR OF MUSIC

It is very important for everyone involved in the music ministry to be on the same page when implementing praise and worship. For numerous reasons we will employ people from varied denominational backgrounds often time specifically because of their skill. Though skillful, it is possible for them to be confused or ignorant when pertaining to praise and worship and may need to be taught in this area.

This is a mistake that would be best not to make. When they lack the knowledge their idea of praise and worship could be totally different from your expectations. If this is not made clear before they are brought in there can be insurmountable problems, confusion and total upset in the music ministry.

This is not to downplay a skillful musician because being proficient is also of utmost importance. Should praise and worship weigh heavy in your service, being sensitive to the Spirit and a musician being able to flow spiritually or prophetically, especially during worship is very essential.

Open communication, mutual respect and humility are critical. Should there be a breakdown in the lines of communication this can create spiritual disconnection during the praise and worship and chaos within the music ministry.

John 10:10

The thief cometh not, but for to steal, and to kill, and to destroy: I am come that they might have life, and that they might have [it] more abundantly.

The enemy does not want our services to be spiritually effective. Where there is foolishness, confusion, rebellion and disrespect he has done, what it is his job to do: steal, kill and destroy. To disrupt the spiritual flow means no getting to God. Thief implies deception and trickery; robber implies violence and destruction. These take away life but Jesus gives life and He gives it abundantly. It is important that the atmosphere be conducive and set for worship. God has given us the power to override the disruptive plans of the enemy.

Tradition must also be considered. If there is a long history of congregational or devotional singing, as mentioned earlier the seasoned members must be considered when changing from that to praise and worship and combining the two will prove ineffective. It would be like playing a game of basketball on a football field.

To experience or generate continued growth, change may be necessary. Religion is not important but relationship with the Father is. When we know better we can do better. I am not implying that you throw out your history or that your way of service is incorrect. But when implementing praise and worship, change is going to be necessary.

People are creatures of habit and congregations seem to enjoy doing the same things, the same way all the time. Whenever change is implemented there usually will be some opposition. When we do things decently and in order topped with a spirit of excellence for the right purpose God will be our buffer.

The head of the music ministry needs to have the same requirements and characteristics of the praise and worship leader, musicians and praise team members. Degrees nor titles should never be used to override order and the authority of the Word of God.

It is important they:

- ❖ Be saved.

- ❖ Be thoroughly trained under someone who is knowledgeable of the fundamentals of music and spiritual flow of the house as well as the importance of praise and worship - a mentor.

- ❖ Be HUMBLE. The Lord thought praise and worship was so important when he created the heavens, He created an angel for this very purpose. This angel was caught up in his own looks and sound till pride overcame him, and he soon believed he was greater than God. Humility had taken flimsy wings and flown out of there. After which God took this angel, that felt he was so wonderful, and all his cronies, and banished them from heaven. This angel's name was Lucifer. Stay humble.

- ❖ Be filled with the Holy Spirit
- ❖ Have a lifestyle pleasing to God.
- ❖ Have an active prayer life. (More than just blessing your food).
- ❖ Study the Word of God (the Bible). Attend Bible Study.
- ❖ BE A TITHER. (Goes to our obedience).
- ❖ Always be on time.
- ❖ Praise and worship should be a lifestyle

Spiritual compromise in any area is a recipe for failure. God will supply who we need to help facilitate pure worship to him so it has the propensity to be acceptable. Remember, it is not a competition.

Philippians 4:19

But my God shall supply all your need according to his riches in glory by Christ Jesus.

Since there is no lack in God's riches in glory we can surmise there is no lack in God's supply. Notice also that this promise is made to the Philippians who had surrendered their finances and material possessions to God's service, and who knew how to give with the right kind of heart. This promise also expresses what Jesus said in Luke 6:38:

Give, and it will be given to you: good measure, pressed down, shaken together, and running over will be put into your bosom. For with the same measure that you use, it will be measured back to you.

God's provisions are conditional but provisions just the same. When we want to present our best God makes a way for our best to be given.

Chapter Six

WORSHIP LEADER

The Praise and worship leader is one of the most intricate people involved in the praise and worship experience. This person is responsible for knowing their craft well enough to facilitate or lead the congregation into the throne room of God.

It is also important that they possess leadership abilities and be knowledgeable of the difference between praise and worship songs. Should your ministry flow prophetically or in the Spirit the leader needs to be familiar with that anointing to avoid a spiritual clash.

The leader usually selects the music and needs to be spiritually sensitive when the Spirit of God is moving. Selecting a leader by talent only can result in them adversely changing the worship atmosphere by being too preachy between songs when they should be exhorting. The spirit of humility helps them to focus and flow allowing God to reign in the service.

There are various genres of worship music and it should be selected according the needs of your particular house. In the early years of my worship experience my former pastor was the musician and worship leader and this gave him a great advantage. As a musician and song writer he could adjust arrangements to enhance his congregation's style of worship music. As our congregation grew and his pastoral responsibilities increased he relinquished the responsibility to his capable wife and co-pastor and they continue to present worship that produces worshippers today.

Again, I emphasize the importance of the following characteristics for the praise and worship leader. The leader does not have to be the best singer in the church but they must:

- ❖ Be saved

- ❖ Familiar with the rudiments and fundamentals of music

- Be thoroughly trained under someone who is knowledgeable of the fundamentals of music and spiritual flow of the house as well as the importance of praise and worship - a mentor.

- Being able to maintain pitch and tonality is important

- Be able to recognize when the pitch or tone is flat or sharp with the team

- Be HUMBLE.

- Be filled with the Holy Spirit

- Living a lifestyle pleasing to God.

- Have an active prayer life. (More than just blessing your food).

- Study the Word of God (the Bible) and attend Bible Study

- BE A TITHER. (Goes to our obedience).

- Always be on time.

- Be in right standing in their church.

- Understand what should and should not be done in Praise and Worship.

- Be an exhorter. *(Exhorter: One who has the ability to give encouragement or incite through scriptural or God given language. To urge strongly through the unction of the Holy Ghost/Holy Spirit; can truly enhance the "Worship" phase and help sustain a worship atmosphere.*

> Every Praise and Worship leader will not develop the gift of exhorting at the beginning of their leadership. If this is the case, they should not attempt to do more than you are capable. Just flow from song to song and let the Lord do the rest. Do not try to promote a gift of preaching. Your purpose is to promote everything as going to God. Make sure you are glorifying God and not glorifying or exalting self.

- ❖ Know the songs thoroughly. We make the congregation uncomfortable when they perceive we do not know what we are doing. Do not sing songs that are too wordy. Remember this is not a time to promote a concert atmosphere. Make it as easy as possible for the audience and you will find a greater participation and receptivity from the people of God.

The character and integrity of a worship leader, the person who facilities the praise and worship is as important as that of the pastor or any leader. Though some do, it is not acceptable to drink and club on Saturday night; to fornicate and satisfy the flesh and expect God to receive your worship with His presence. What we have here is merely talent or gifting without the anointing which is merely an exercise.

Quality rehearsal time, self-preparation, harmony and techniques and being cognizant of the spiritual needs of the attending worshippers are important.

The worship leader does not need to have the best voice but should be able to maintain tonality. Leading worship is different from singing a solo or lead to a song.

One must first know the difference between praise and worship so as not to confuse the congregants by asking them to "praise and worship" simultaneously. We can only do one at a time successfully.

It is not the worship leader's responsibility to neither prompt or prime people nor be preachy between song selections. Do what you are called to do and lead the praise and worship portion of the service.

The leader may be inspired by the Spirit of God to flow in a "new" song but not arbitrarily create songs, unless they are truly flowing in and with the Spirit of God. This requires spiritual maturity and sensitivity. If it is not spirit birthed the atmosphere of worship will become diluted.

Leaders should recognize once the pastor resumes the pulpit they should follow their lead because they now become the facilitator. There should never be a time where it seems to be a battle with the worship leader and one of the team or either with the pastor. It is NOT ABOUT YOU! When we try to fabricate a move of God the moment becomes spiritually chaotic and disconnected.

I am reminded years ago, when our young adult choir introduced drums, the electric piano, tambourine, clapping and choreographed choral movements and other instruments to our morning service. People were offended and oftentimes did not receive the choir because this tremendously changed the music of our services. There were no warnings or teachings presented regarding the implemented addition in our music but suddenly, a traditional missionary Baptist Church that only used the instrumentation of a Leslie organ and Baby Grand piano were thrust into what some would call the modern age of Christian contemporary gospel music with an electric piano, drums, bass and various percussion instruments.

Consequently, because of a change in the music, on any given Sunday morning we had the "battle of the saints," choir versus saints each with their own following and supporters within the same church. Instead of congregants being in spiritual warfare against principalities there was chaotic warfare amongst themselves.

It is not wise to implement praise and worship into the service because "everyone is doing it." There should be an understanding of the purpose and the goal should be to corporately get into the presence of God.

Chapter Seven

PRAISE AND WORSHIP TEAM

Though the choir may back the team it is usually separate from the choir but can consist of choir members. It requires a higher level of commitment, additional (separate) rehearsals and persons that display spiritual maturity. Depending on the size of the music ministry the team sometimes serves as both.

As discussed earlier, not all singers or vocalist are praise and worship material. We all have challenges in our Christian walk but those with obvious spiritual struggles are best suited for the choir rather than as a part of the team. Remember, lifestyle is praise and worship so character, integrity and accountability is important and should be part of the criteria used for the selection process.

A large number of our twenty-first century ministries do not enforce any specific dress code. This is good so that people can feel comfortable in wearing what they have. On the contrary, leadership, including the praise and worship team should be required to dress appropriately as not to be a distraction. Short, tightfitting, revealing clothing is inappropriate. Members learn what appropriate attire is by watching the example the staff and leaders set before them.

Pastors and leaders must remember everything that is sold in a store is not appropriate for service. Stretch pants, clinging or sheer tops, clothing that appears too small; I am sure you have a visual idea by now. The club and the world accept anything, but God wants our best and it should be presented with a spirit of excellence.

It is important that the ministry of praise and worship maintains an atmosphere which can usher in the presence of God. People walking, being seated, trying to be seen all are huge distractions. Have you ever been at the entrance of the throne room and someone taps you on the shoulder, or people are entering and exiting the pulpit area? Not only is this a distraction, but to a true worshipper it can be very irritating.

Another important element to be considered by the team is everyone on the team does not need to adlib. This will be conceived as a battle of the voices. Never over power the leader. Lastly, worship leaders and the team should arrive before service time. This allows time to do a sound check, pray together, make necessary adjustments and to become spiritually focused.

The "praise and worship Team" was ordained and instituted way back in the Old Testament, and some of the same practices that were essential in the worship services then, are essential today.

The following are some standard instructions for anyone desiring to be on a Praise and Worship Team:

- ❖ Should be willing to train under their qualified praise and worship leader who (is hopefully) knowledgeable of the fundamentals and rudiments of music and familiar with flowing in the Spirit. They too should know the importance and difference between "praise and worship." Be mentored.

- ❖ Must be saved.

- ❖ Must live a lifestyle pleasing to God.

- ❖ Must have an active prayer life.

- ❖ Must study the Word of God (attend Bible Study).

- ❖ Must be in good standing in their church.

- ❖ Must understand what is acceptable and what is unacceptable during "Praise and Worship."

- ❖ Must know the songs thoroughly.

- ❖ MUST BE A TITHER AND A GIVER. (Goes to our obedience).

- ❖ Never play or wave or make faces or gestures to the other members of the team or the congregation.

- ❖ Must always be on time. God is counting on us.

- ❖ Must be a able and willing to follow leadership.

Lastly, understanding the purpose of praise and worship in our service, the team should not "cheer on" any leader of a song, during this time this is very appropriate. But it is a great gesture for choir members to "cheer on" the leader of a song during choir selections, but NEVER during the praise and worship period.

Chapter Eight

MUSICIANS

Musicians are another intricate part of the praise and worship experience. They are responsible for knowing their craft well enough to play with others while accompanying the praise leader and team. They do not have to be the best musicians but should be knowledgeable of the fundamentals and rudiments of music as well as the art of praise and worship. To play skillfully is not necessarily playing loud. If the team and leader cannot be heard above the instruments they are probably playing too loud.

Some present day musicians seem to exempt themselves from structure and order. The idea appears, to see just how far one can push the envelope. It is not unusual for them to be notoriously late, wearing sports attire, playing unnecessary distracting augmented chord structures, playing excessively loud and lacking discernment.

It's wonderful to have skilled musicians but they also need to know how to musically flow prophetically or in the spirit during worship. They should be held to the same standards and requirements as the worship leader and team listed in the preceding chapters.

Acts 2:1

And when the day of Pentecost was fully come, they were all with one accord in one place.

When the leader, team and musicians work **with** one accord it means they are together sharing the same heart, the same love for God, the same trust in His promise, as they share the same space.

To all Senior Pastors, God gave you the vision for the work in your house and appointed you as shepherd. Sometimes workers forget who is in charge. Before bringing something into your worship service, be comfortable and sure you understand and agree with it.

Once praise and worship is established never allow yourself to become so busy or involved that you neglect the integrity of the praise and worship in your house.

Proverbs 4:7

Wisdom is the principal thing; therefore get wisdom: and with all thy getting get understanding

First, get wisdom, get understanding and *with all thy getting, get understanding.* Pray for it, take pains for it, and give diligence in the use of all appointed means to attain it. Wait at wisdom's gate as in Proverbs 8:34.

Blessed is the man that heareth me, watching daily at my gates, waiting at the posts of my doors.

This next statement is not meant to be disrespectful. It is important when pastoring family, and if they are going to serve in any leadership capacity, they are required to meet the same standards and requirements as any member in leadership. Too often dissention manifests and a churches growth is stunted by a close relative or immediate family member receiving preferential treatment.

Chapter Nine

PRAISE AND WORSHIP SERVICE

What an experience to be in such deep worship that you actually feel the Shekinah glory and presence of God. It is that moment in time when those that don't have a clue are weeping and those that do are entering in. Worship carries you into a place in God that can exclude the need for a message; a time of worship in which God has done a work in and through the entire congregation.

There will always be an unexplainable gratitude for my introduction to praise and worship and for the sound teaching and the actual experience. It was in my adult life that I first encountered a true move of God during praise and worship that was not based solely on emotions. Having this experience is noble and dangerous because the sensitivity developed for true worship is ever so compelling.

All that is shared in this book has been from a biblical perspective, personal experience and from sound teaching and research over many years. Though it is not my intention to cast dispersions on any ministry, if we compromise and lose sight of the purpose of praise and worship we miss the mark.

Many have veered from spiritually powerful representation to the team and leader wearing inappropriate clothing and the practice of ungodly lifestyles (told by pictures and comments plastered on social media). A gross lack of spiritual maturation and the shepherd seemingly looking the other way while making excuses for the incongruous, all fuels meaningless, manufactured experiences and the overall ineffectiveness of many worship services.

We also have those who are thrust into the position because they have a lovely voice and yet lack the spiritual maturity and knowledge of the responsibility of being a praise and worship leader. Many have not lived long enough to develop a believable lifestyle of holiness. Mimicking is not difficult but living it should cost us something. As they use to say, we use people that are still "wet behind the ears."

It is so much more rewarding and perceptible when one is a true worshipper, living the lifestyle rather than one who learns the gestures and trendy phrasing as they mimic other artist.

All need to be sensitive to the Spirit of God. When operating in the flesh it can cause major distractions by simply talking at the wrong time, or changing the music prematurely which causes one to simply miss the spiritual flow.

Should praise and worship be coupled with devotion or you want to introduce praise and worship into your worship services, it is wise to transition with teaching so the introduction can be smooth. Sound teaching on praise and worship and the proposed change will be necessary to help educate all ages. It will also help make the transition for seniors and mature congregants that are accustomed to devotional or congregational singing get involved and be receptive. Presenting devotion and praise and worship at the same time is ineffective.

Whether you are the pastor, worship team leader or lay-member, proper training which includes biblical instructions and spiritual motivation will take this period of your service to a higher dimension.

Setting the Atmosphere

Once we understand the purpose of our praise and worship, and develop trained leaders, teams and musicians and put them into place we can present God our best.

During the praise and worship a person being seated during praise is tolerable depending upon your media set-up and available area for waiting. But during worship seating, walking (including in the pulpit) should come to a halt. There are several ways this can be reinforced:

1. After proper teaching an announcement should be made and printed in the program of your target date, and fliers made available to congregants regarding the change and when to expect its implementation. Members will make an effort to be on time or they will experience remaining outside until

worship has ended. My experience over the years is members that are truly chasing after God develop a sincere consciousness for time.

2. Make sure the porters are aware there is to be **NO** seating during worship nor should there be any walking from those already seated. They will also need training so they can be diplomatic with those that resist.

3. Since we encounter visitors and seasonal members from week to week, it is good to place the following statement in your weekly bulletin:

"In respect to God and other worshippers, please refrain from walking during praise and worship. Please be advised during the worship portion of service no one will be seated or allowed to exit. Thank you."

Praise and worship should not be viewed as a trend, scripture proves this. True holiness should secretes one's integrity and character and is not a prerequisite inasmuch as it is a required and developed daily lifestyle.

When we can absorb the truth deep within our spirit and then exemplify it in our worship service it will not be necessary for it to be fabricated. We were created to worship God. The Word compels and constrains us to worship God.

Psalm 66:4

All the earth shall worship You And sing praises to You; They shall sing praises to Your name." Selah

The psalmist is calling upon all people to praise God. This alludes to the Glory of God and that He is worthy to be praised. It is a part of the law of creation that and is required of every creature.

Everything can praise God but not all can worship. In praise, the heavens declare Him, the earth implores Him and man celebrates

Him. Only man can partake in worship because it must be done in spirit (only significant to man) and in truth only accessible by man.

Chapter Ten

PRAISE AND WORSHIP ENHANCEMENTS

<u>Eliminate Distractions</u>

All of this may seem trivial and it is if getting into the presence of God is not relevant for your ministry or is not your spiritual goal. In reviewing the history of the pulpit the size of the pulpit and its overelaborate carvings was to emphasize the Word, as if the Word was coming from God, and not to cast attention on the preacher.

Before the church had pulpits scrolls were read to a seated congregation while the teacher stood and read because of the length and bulkiness of the scroll.

The elevation of the pulpit seems to symbolize the elevated stature of the scriptures and not the preacher. In the pulpit area the enemy uses distraction to interrupt our worship experience. When people are entering and exiting the pulpit area during worship, spectators and true worshippers will both be distracted and lose focus blocking any possibility for a successful, corporate worship experience.

Should this be a problem during your worship experience it is easily remedied. When members of the congregation know what is; and is not acceptable behavior, they react accordingly. When we know better we can do better.

Under no circumstance should the praise and worship leader, team or choir members chew gum. With most of our services being taped for viewing or commercial use it is not a good media look. Some people suffer with dry mouth and need something in their mouth or water on hand to counter-act that symptom but gum should not be chewed.

<u>Be Lyric Conscious</u>

Distinguish a praise song from a worship song by the <u>lyrics</u> not by the <u>rhythm</u> (slow or fast). Review Chapter One for clarification.

Be mindful of word diction or enunciation:
 a. Wor-ship **not** Wor-shup
 b. Hea-ven **not** Hea-vun
 c. Pre-sence **not** pre-sunce
 d. You **not** chew
 e. Emphasize endings on your words especially words ending in D, S, and T.

Just because a song is recorded or published by a well-known artist and every church in the country is singing it, does not make it conducive for your service or authenticate it to be biblically correct. Do your homework.

Try to refrain from always doing what is popular but instead do what is powerful. Popular can be good because people are usually familiar but empowering is much more productive and spiritually rewarding.

Perfect the Sound

Avoid giving lead microphones to singers that have trouble with "pitch." When using omnidirectional microphones everyone must have good pitch. Put in the rehearsal time needed to produce a quality sound.

There is nothing worse than being in the audience and having your hearing bruised because you have to listen around a sharp soprano or a flat alto or tenor.

Use Media

Posting the lyrics on giant screens is effective, especially for new converts in your congregation. But there is some legality you must consider:

 a. List the recording artist name
 b. If you must use tracks as an accompaniment make sure they are instrumental only.

It is so important that we avail our ministries to laws that govern the church. As much as we would like to think we are above the law, we are not. From a legal standpoint apply for Church Copyright License (CCL).

The Purpose

The copyright law is very clear on copying music. If you do not have permission from the rightful owner of the song you cannot make copies. This law is fair but not practical because getting permission can be time consuming.

CCL is a contractual agreement with songwriters and publishers of over 200,000 songs. For an annual fee the church receives permission to copy songs. The license is nontransferable (cannot be shared).

This legally allows the printing of songs, lyrics and hymns in a bulletin or program and projecting transparencies and slides. For your service to be legally recorded whether audio or video it should be presented with live music. Accompaniment tracks cannot be reproduced. (CCLI.com)

Synopsis

Undoubtedly, some will be of the opinion that praise and worship does not require all of this and everyone is entitled to their opinion. But as you draw your conclusion, remember the purpose of this book is not to just be influential but moreover to share information, educate and give constructive insight so you might have a phenomenal worship experience.

For some, this information may be the norm for your church worship experience and for others change may be needed. You may also be thinking this requires too much work and effort.

Whatever is concluded, agreed or disagreed with, chasing after God is a worthwhile effort which proves itself over time as we press daily to get into His presence. This does not take anything away from what is already established but it propels us to an almost indefinable and intangible spiritual dimension in God.

Those who were able to establish their church service with this kind of praise and worship anointing from its conception are truly blessed. The consensus is usually they too were mentored for a season and began establishing the atmosphere for an encounter with God.

We must also be careful not to take visitations from God for granted, or allow ourselves to become unfocused and distracted often changing things to compete with whatever is trendy or deemed the norm. This I have personally experienced. Somehow flesh eases into the equation as though they never saw it coming. Unfortunately, what was once a haven with an open door conducive for entering into the presence of God becomes a service time of entertainment.

Shepherds guard your sheep well, praise and worship teams and leaders learn your craft, musicians remember it is the anointing that destroys yokes to all remember, true worship is a lifestyle.

About the Author

Shiela Y. Harris

Shiela Harris is a songwriter, motivational-speaker, preacher of the Gospel, life coach, poet and author who has a strong deliverance ministry for women. For a short while she served as a volunteer writer for the Antelope Valley Community Newspaper, "Antelope Valley Sentinel."

Shiela received her Bachelor of Art from California State University, Dominguez Hills (Cum Laude) and to further equip her for ministry she attended the Southern California School of Ministry (First Church of God Inglewood Campus) receiving a Masters in Ministry (Cum Laude) and was one of the commencement speakers.

Currently she is a member of Worship Center Community Church, Long Beach, California. She believes her purpose is to be a writer/teacher/preacher and to dedicate her life to the task God has set before her, ministering to women helping them reach a place of divine wholeness and wellness in God, grief support, church administration, staff training and more. Her writings are influenced by personal experiences coupled with biblical principles and research. People want and need truths. For this and other reasons, she is transparent as she often uses life's mistakes and accomplishments to inform, encourage, empower and cause change.

Booking Agent-Eva J.
http://www.touchingtheworldnow.com

About Roosevelt Theodore Harris III

Affectionately known to everyone as **Pastor Ted**, he was married to Shiela Y. Harris for eleven years. Although called to preach the Gospel his greatest love in ministry for many years was music. He was an accomplished song writer and has over 200 gospel tunes to his credit. He was also founder of the renowned gospel group, the "Inspirational Voices of Praise" (I.V.O.P.) that has a vinyl album to their credit titled, "You Can Make It." All songs were written and produced by Ted Harris; musical arrangements were by Ted Harris and Darrell Alston.

Pastor Ted had a rich background in Church music, having been exposed to some of the finest exponents of gospel music. After serving a long apprenticeship with Dr. Rodena Preston and The Voices of Deliverance, he inspired to venture on his own and display all of his own inspiration and ideas of what good contemporary gospel music should be. His music never lost the concept of gospel music, which is the message of Christ, and His love for all.

Pastor Ted was also founder of the "The Gospel Music and Instructional Workshop," which met annually for 15 years. He used the workshop as a channel to teach choir decorum, vocal drills and the rudiments and fundamentals of music to choir members, choir directors and musicians. The workshop also opened a door for new artist to introduce new music. As a choir director, vocal coach and percussionist, he has sang and been affiliated with some of gospels greatest: The late Rev. James Cleveland, Dr. Rodena Preston (Voices of Deliverance), John P. Kee, Prof. Stan Lee, Robert Gilmore and many more.

Ted loved to teach the art of praise and worship. He studied it extensively and taught the subject to numerous choirs in many venues. He was working on this book, an in depth study of the art of praise and worship when his battle with a reoccurring illness halted the work. Ted was a man of order and excellence and strongly believed order allows us to give excellence back to God.

"The shame isn't in not knowing but in knowing that you don't know and not trying to find out."

G.M.I.W. MOTTO

When we Get it right – We Can Get to God

Other Teaching Topics:

*How to be Free from Excess Baggage

For all whom take (knowingly and unknowingly) unresolved, emotional issues from one relationship to another. Life's negative experiences resulting from traumas encountered in childhood and as adults are destructive and result in low and no self-esteem. Ultimately this often results in chaotic, dysfunctional relationships. This book teaches the why and how we take painful experiences into new relationships better known as "excess baggage," and how to get delivered from its weight as you are made free and know it. A powerful deliverance ministry.

*Ladies, No More Fishing

This is a dynamic teaching targeting women who are seeking God for a mate. Learn how to control the flesh and successfully live single while you wait for your mate. Biblical and practical principles are used encouraging women to wait on God because when we fish for men we set ourselves up for destructive, unfulfilled, one-sided relationships.

Do Christians Have to Fall

There are many great men and women who have been tricked and fooled by the enemy. Secretly and in the open they are caught up in ungodly and sinful practices that not only discredits them, but also the Body of Christ. This teaching helps us to understand how and why we fall and also biblically supports that we do not have to fall, and moreover how to keep from falling.

*I'm Grieving and I Can't Get Up

Teaching based on the book, "Surviving the Loss of a Loved One." We learn how to understand the grieving process, what to expect during grieving and how to survive it. She transparently shares the loss of her husband after eleven years of marriage and her emotional rollercoaster ride throughout the grieving process. This can be very beneficial to your congregation to help those who are caught in the grieving cycle, to go through in a healthy manner and come out healthy and victorious. Also teaches us how to recognize danger symptoms, knowing what to do when we experience "melt downs" and where to look for additional help if needed.

Ministering to Your Pastor

Biblical principles for and the importance of parishioners financially supporting their ministry and pastor. Biblical reference to the ministry of tithes and offerings and what God says about our giving and the importance of pastors living and leading with Character, Integrity and Accountability.

Recipe for a LOVING Marriage

With divorce as common in the church as in the world, practical principles and Biblical teaching on saving the institution of marriage. What causes marriages to fail? Why are spouses unfaithful? Have men and women's rolls switched or changed? Can spouses be faithful? What does the Bible say about Divorce? Why do we fall out of love so easy and more?

*Church Administration & Staff Training

How to perform in an effective and efficient manner using up-to-date technology, forms control, software and uniformed office procedures. Organizing your work, providing ongoing training and managing your staff as you develop 21st Century Leaders.

Signs of an Abusive Relationship & How to Get Out

When God send your rib it should not hurt. Biblical teaching on marriage, divorce and abuse. The dangers of remaining in a physically or emotionally abusive relationship. What the Bible says regarding these issues.

Living Single and Holy While Waiting for Your Mate
How to live single without being promiscuous - Having intimacy without having sex; controlling your flesh and more...

* Publications can be purchased at Amazon.com

TRAINING INFORMATION AND BOOKS ARE ALSO LISTED ON SITES BELOW:

http://churchadministrationtraining.webs.com

Amazon.com
In search box put: Shiela Y. Harris

How to Be Free From Excess Baggage

Surviving the Loss of a Loved One

Ladies No More Fishing

How Does God Choose?

Church Administration – Developing 21st Century Leaders

Short Fictional Stories That May Be True: